This book belongs to:

_____

YOU ARE AMAZING JUST THE WAY YOU ARE.

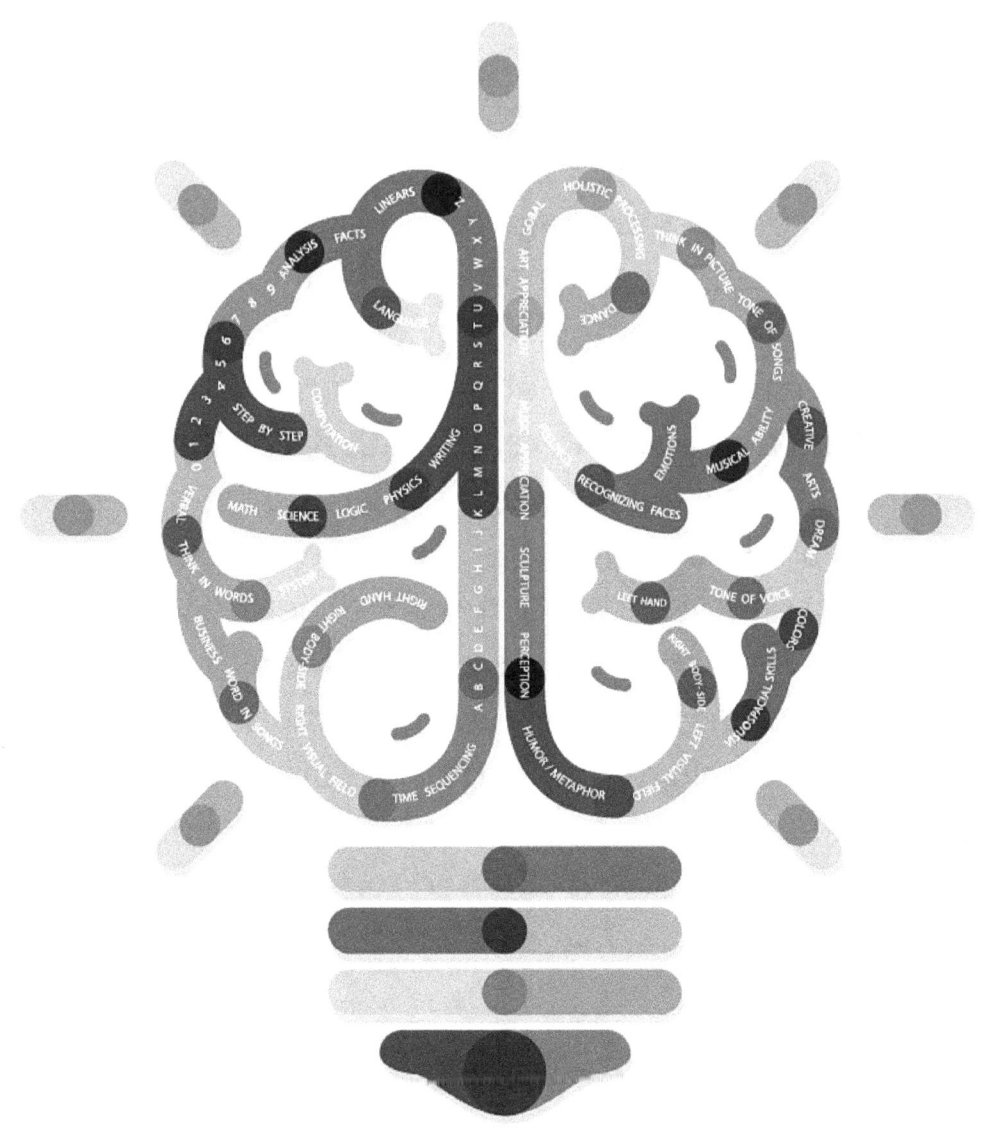

© Copyright 2021-2025- All rights reserved.

You may not reproduce, duplicate or send the contents of this book without direct written permission from the author. You cannot hereby despite any circumstance blame the publisher or hold him or her to legal responsibility for any reparation, compensations, or monetary forfeiture owing to the information included herein, either in a direct or an indirect way.

Legal Notice: This book has copyright protection. You can use the book for personal purpose. You should not sell, use, alter, distribute, quote, take excerpts or paraphrase in part or whole the material contained in this book without obtaining the permission of the author first.

Disclaimer Notice: You must take note that the information in this document is for casual reading and entertainment purposes only. We have made every attempt to provide accurate, up to date and reliable information. We do not express or imply guarantees of any kind. The persons who read admit that the writer is not occupied in giving legal, financial, medical or other advice. We put this book content by sourcing various places.

Please consult a licensed professional before you try any techniques shown in this book. By going through this document, the book lover comes to an agreement that under no situation is the author accountable for any forfeiture, direct or indirect, which they may incur because of the use of material contained in this document, including, but not limited to, —errors, omissions, or inaccuracies.

| Aa | Bb |

Cc Dd

Ee Ff

Gg Hh

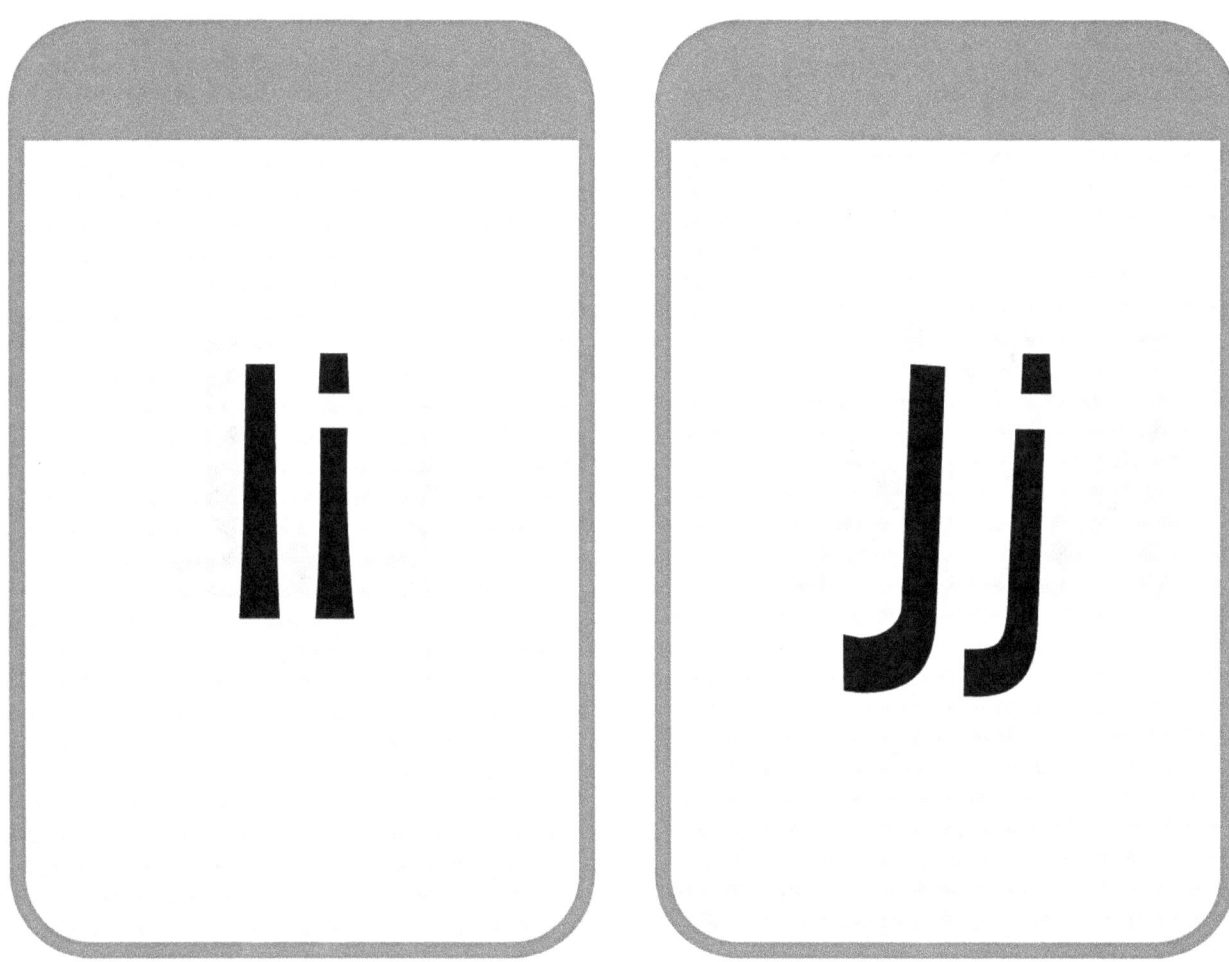

Kk   Ll

Mm Nn

Oo Pp

Qq Rr

Ss Tt

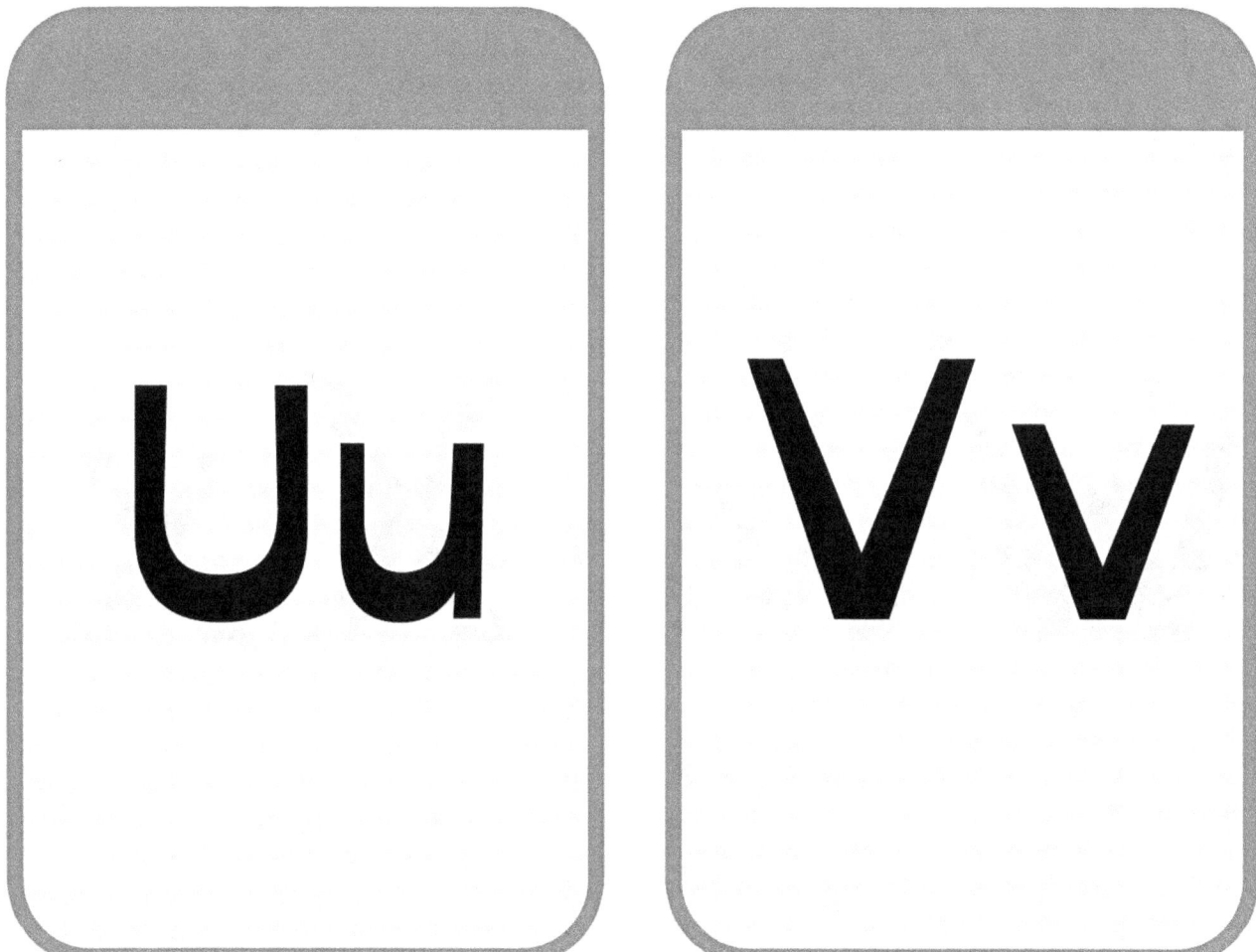

Ww Xx

Yy Zz

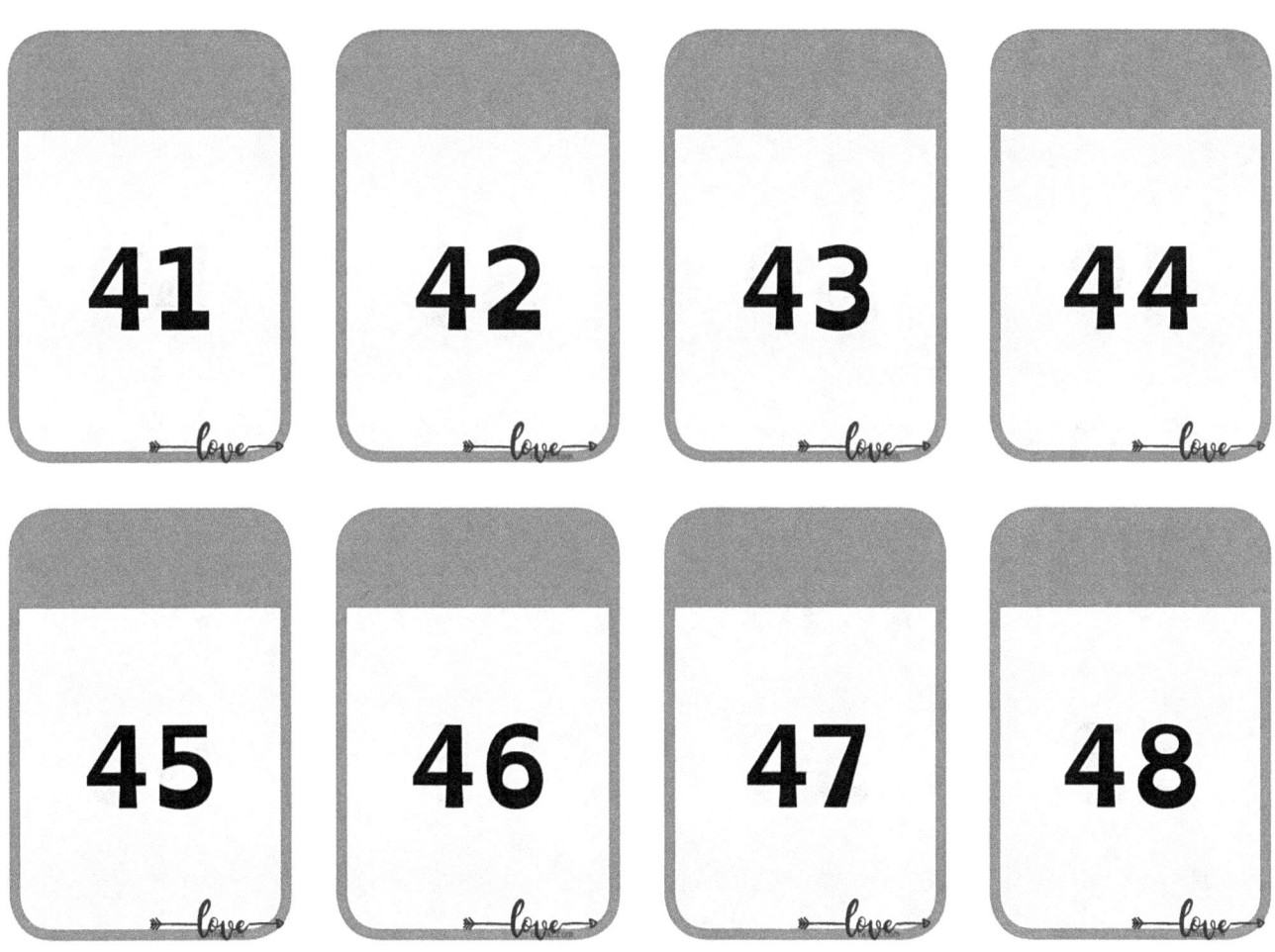

89	90	91	92
93	94	95	96
97	98	99	100

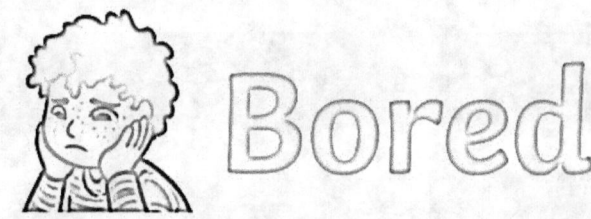

Bored

Colour in the strategies you would use to manage boredom.

When I feel bored, I can feel better by...

playing outside   playing a game with someone from home   drawing a picture

reading a book   doing a jigsaw puzzle   building a den

Add a strategy of your own.

Tired

Colour in the strategies you would use to manage tiredness.

When I feel tired, I can feel better by...

having a rest   reading a book   eating a healthy snack

lying down for a nap   going outside   watching a TV programme

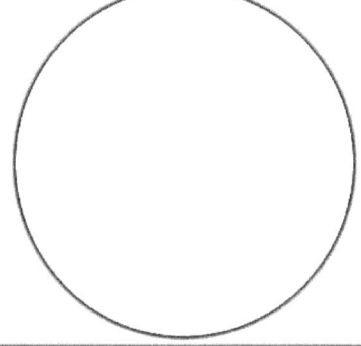

Add a strategy of your own.

# Scared

Colour in the strategies you would use to manage fear.

When I feel scared, I can feel better by...

 talking to someone I trust

 drawing a picture of what I am scared of

 getting an air cuddle

 taking deep breaths

 thinking about something else

 staying close to someone from home

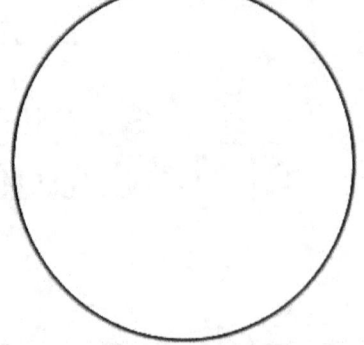

Add a strategy of your own.

Sad

Colour in the strategies you would use to manage sadness.

When I feel sad, I can feel better by...

talking to someone I trust

playing with my favourite toy

getting an air cuddle

drawing a picture

exercising

listening to music

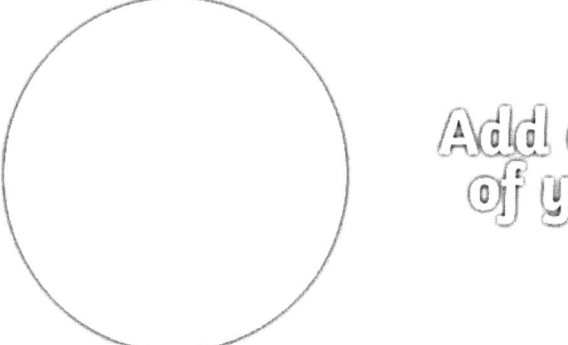

Add a strategy of your own.

Angry

Colour in the strategies you would use to manage anger.

When I feel angry, I can feel better by...

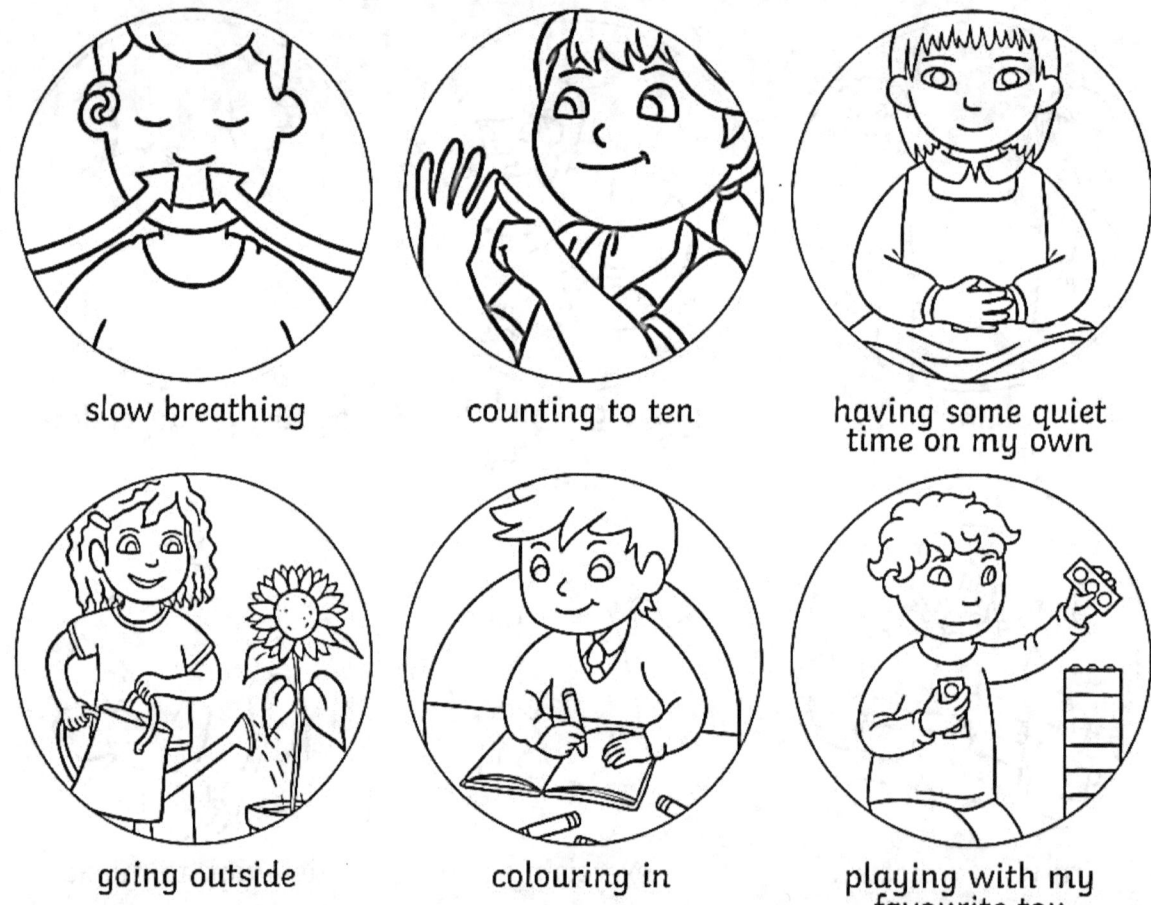

slow breathing   counting to ten   having some quiet time on my own

going outside   colouring in   playing with my favourite toy

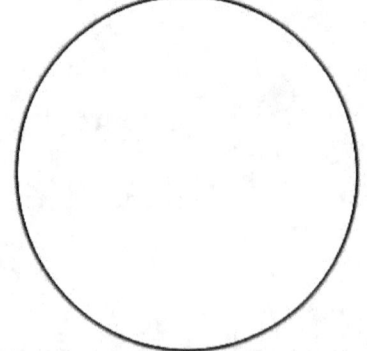

Add a strategy of your own.

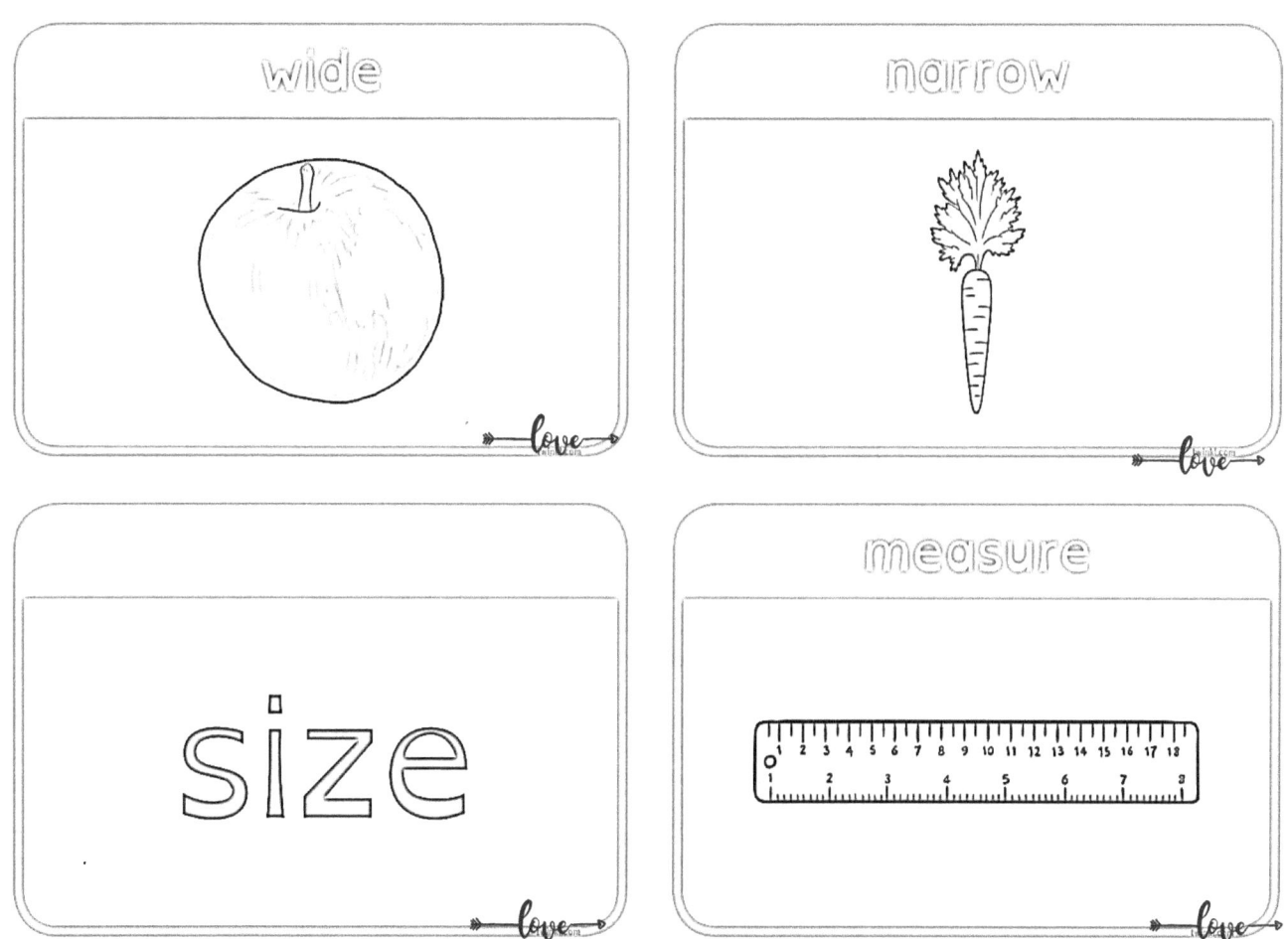

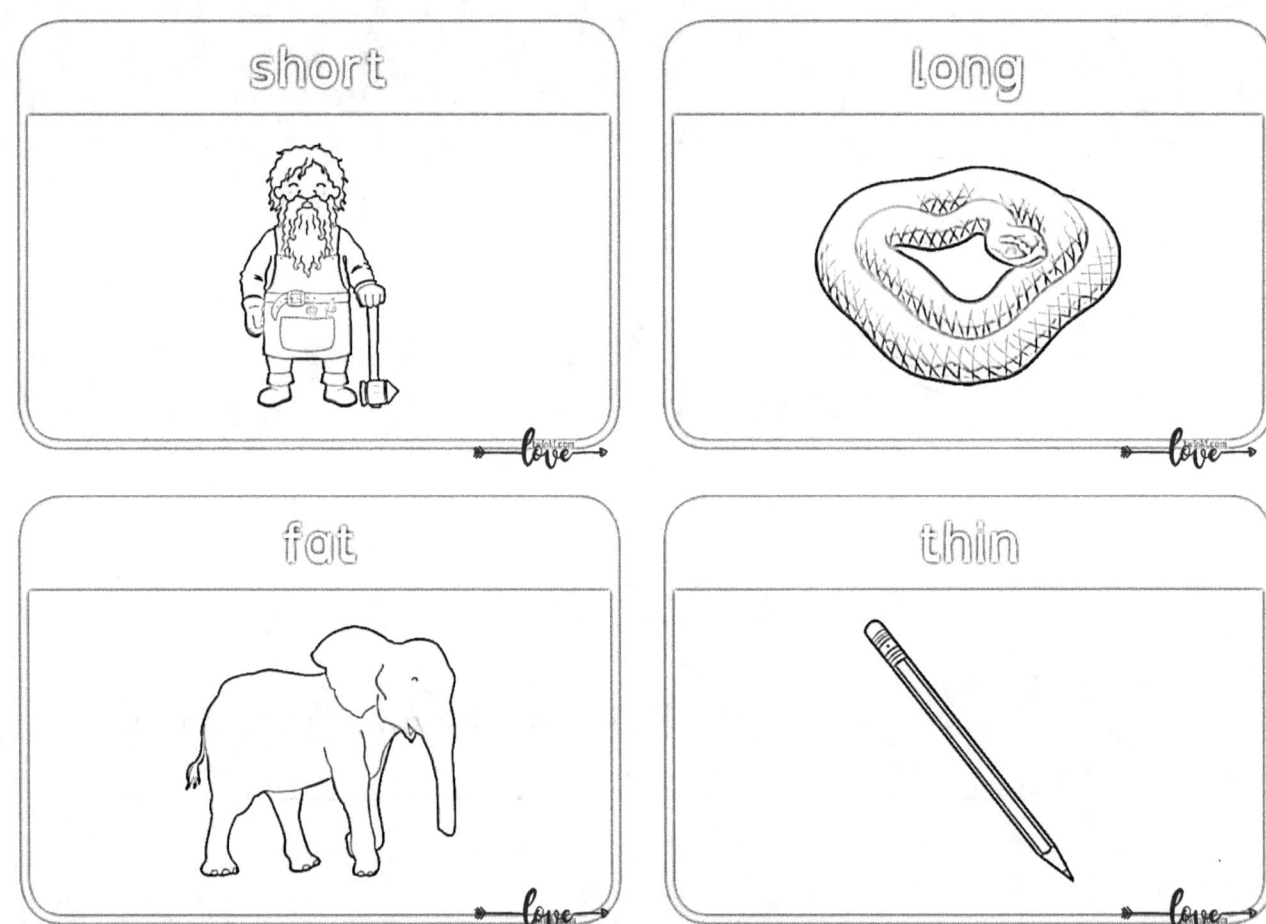

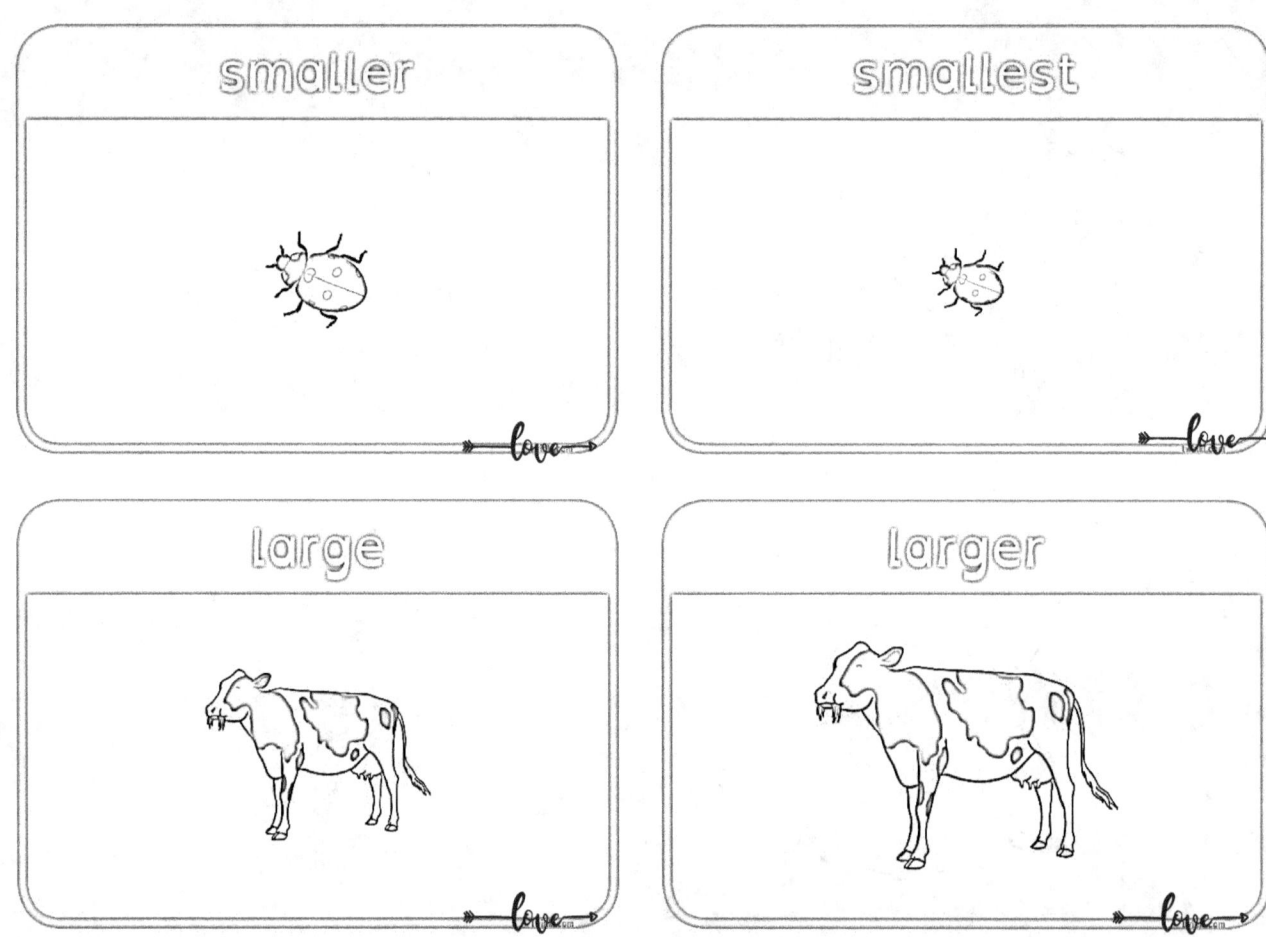

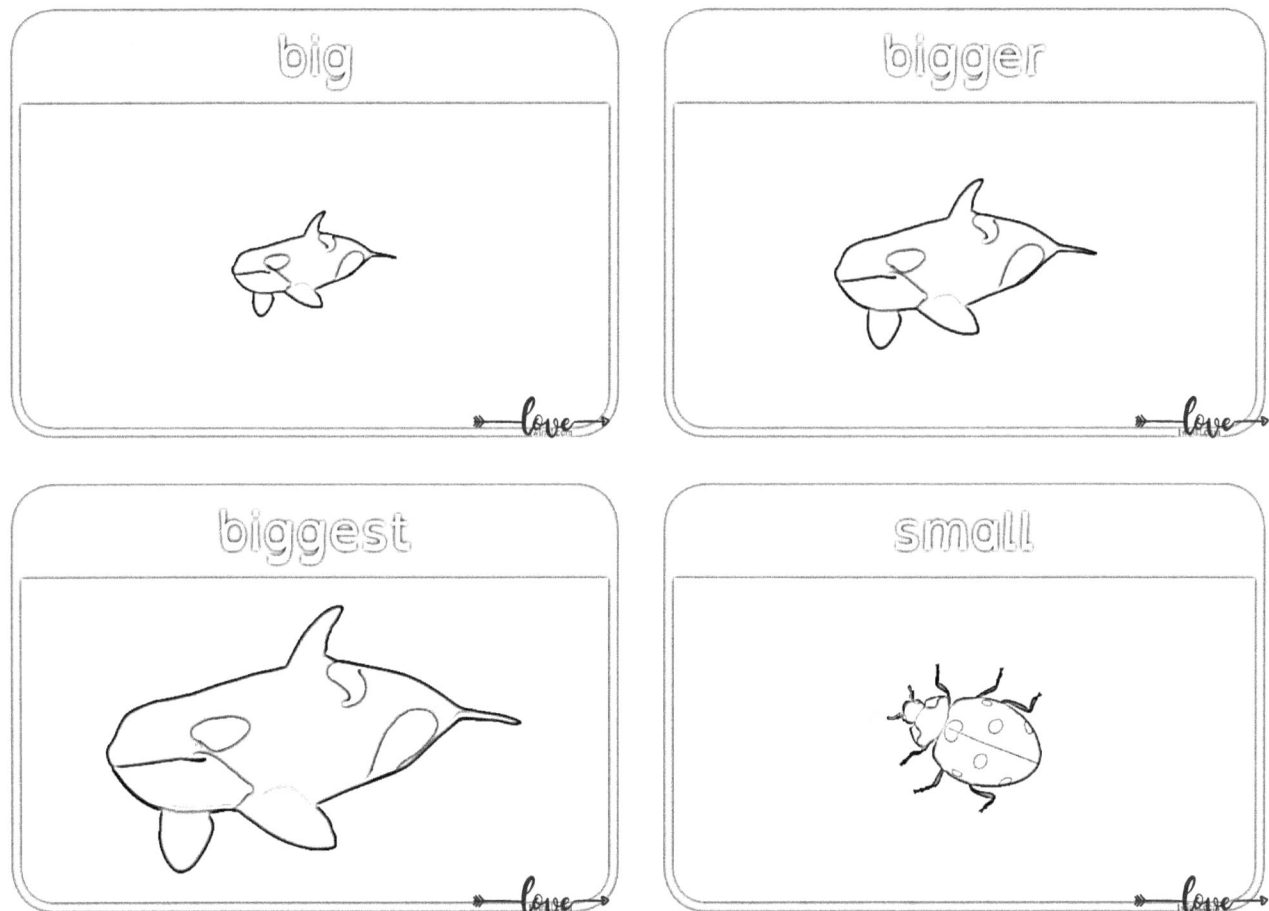

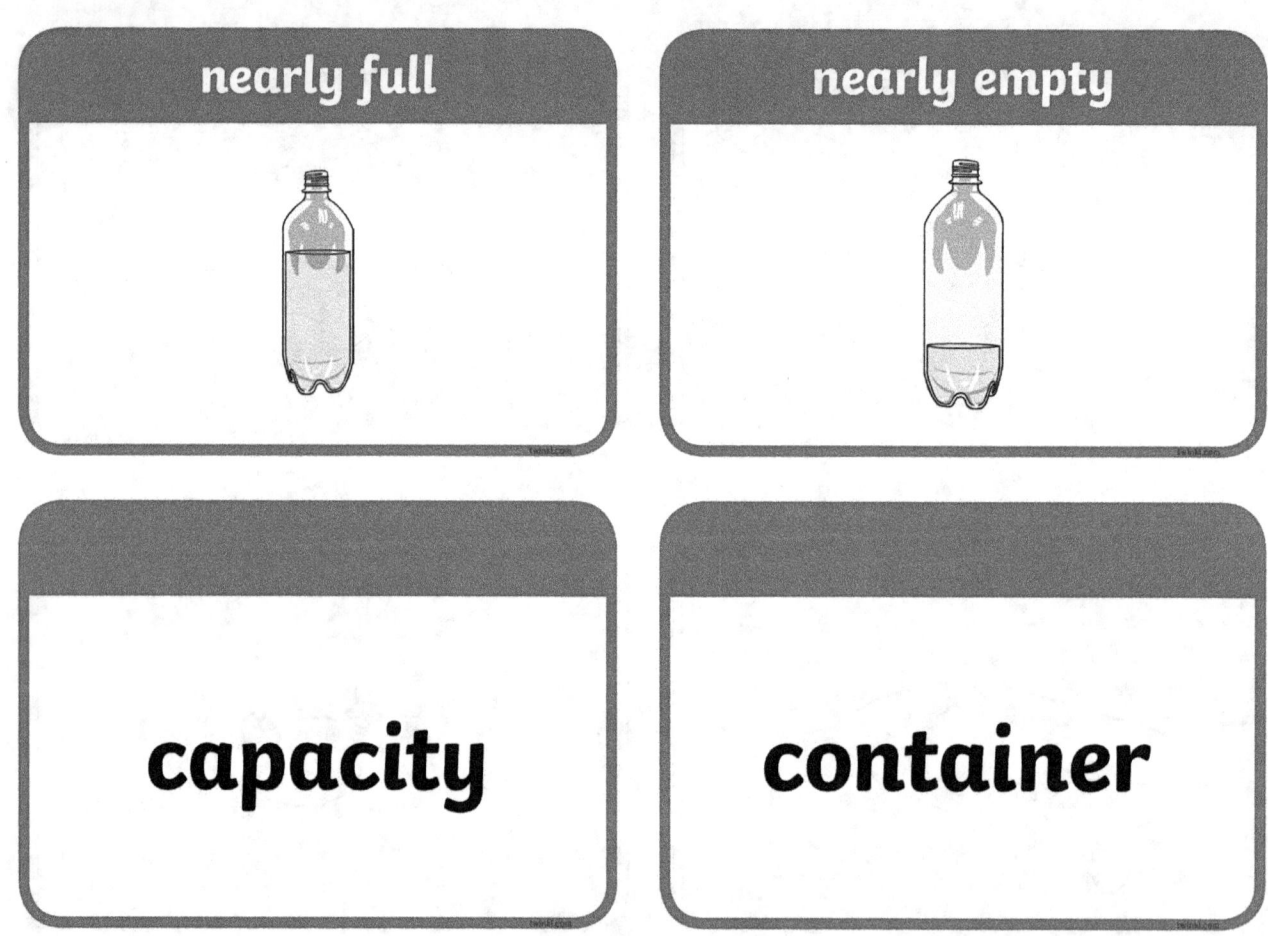

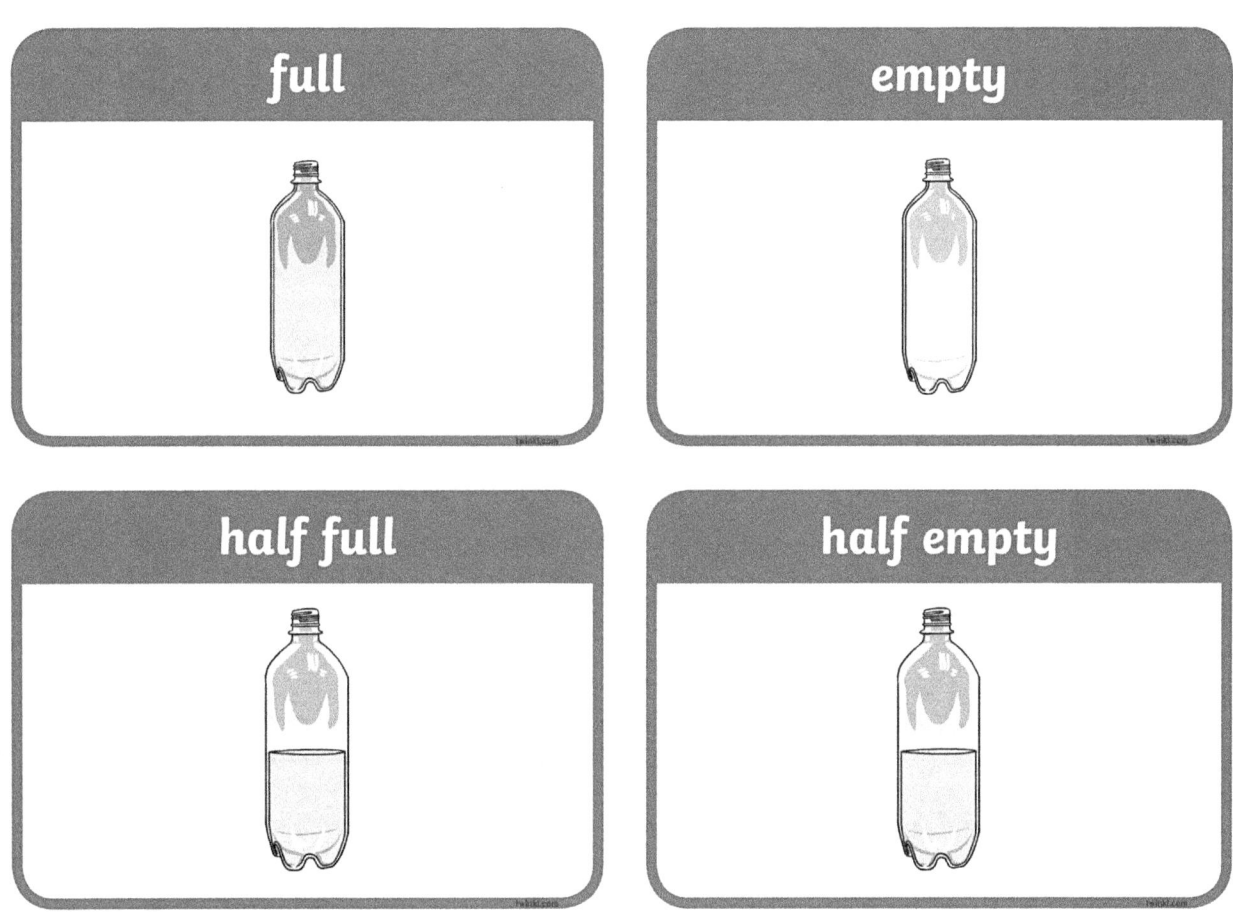

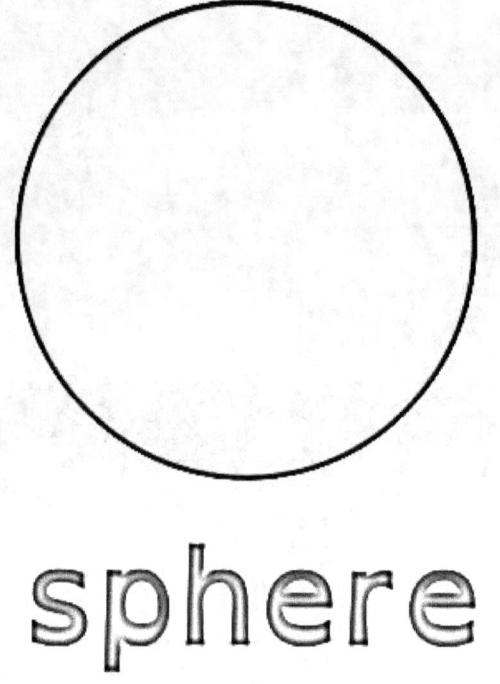
sphere

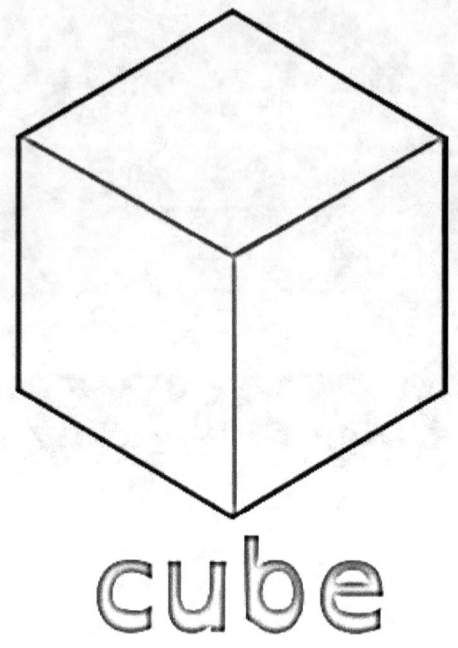
cube

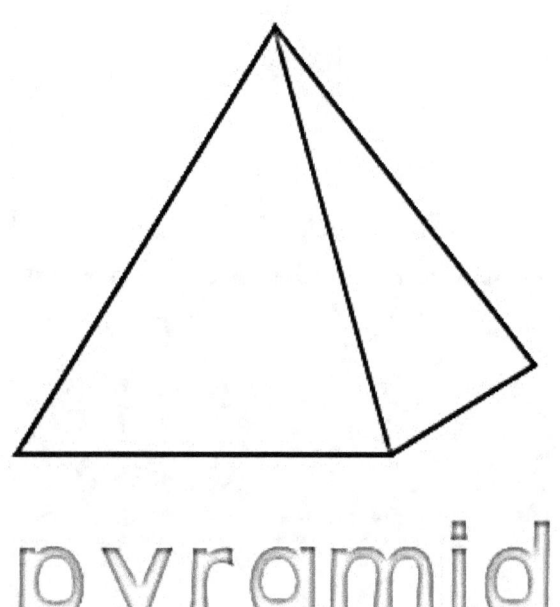
pyramid

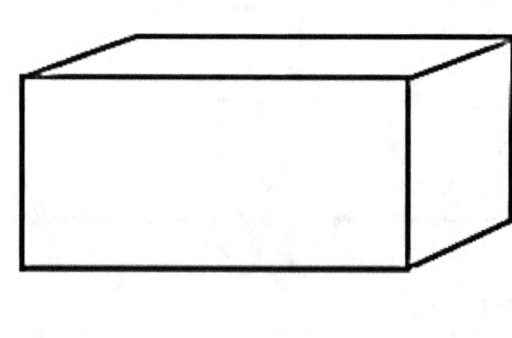
cuboid

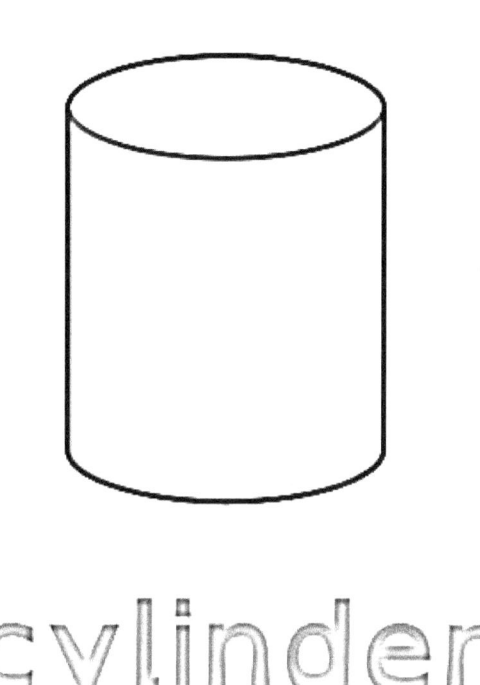

cylinder

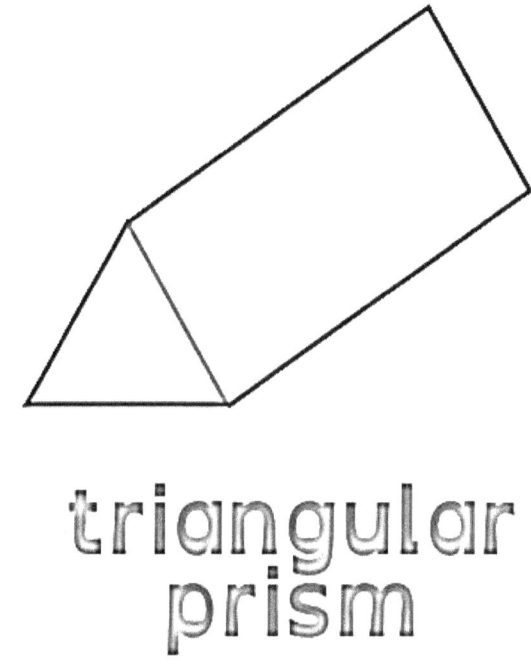

triangular prism

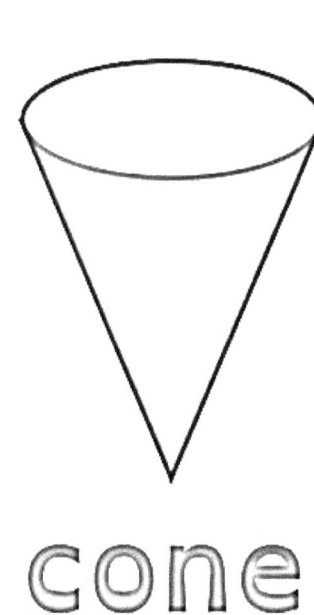

cone

Confusing Letters Colouring Sheet

(b) Colour in blue   (d) Colour in red.

b d d b b d
d d b d b b
b b d b d d
d d b d d b
b b b d b d
d d b d d b

Confusing Letters Colouring Sheet

| (n) Colour in pink | (h) Colour in red. |

n h h h n h
n n h h n h
h h n n n h
h n n h n h
h n n h n h
h h n h n h

Confusing Letters Colouring Sheet

| j Colour in orange. | i Colour in purple. |

j i i j j j
j j i i j i
i j j j i i
j i i i i j
j j i j i i
j i i j i j

Confusing Letters Colouring Sheet

| p | Colour in yellow. | q | Colour in green. |

p q p q q q
p p q p q p
q p p q p q
p p q p q p
q q q p p p
p p q p q q

Confusing Letters Colouring Sheet

| k Colour in blue | R Colour in red. |

R k k R R k
k R R k k R
R k R R k R
k R k R R R
k R R k R k
k R k R R k

100 Square

1	2	3	4	5	6	7	8	9	10
11	12	13	14	15	16	17	18	19	20
21	22	23	24	25	26	27	28	29	30
31	32	33	34	35	36	37	38	39	40
41	42	43	44	45	46	47	48	49	50
51	52	53	54	55	56	57	58	59	60
61	62	63	64	65	66	67	68	69	70
71	72	73	74	75	76	77	78	79	80
81	82	83	84	85	86	87	88	89	90
91	92	93	94	95	96	97	98	99	100

Adverbs

How? (manner)		When? (time)	How often? (frequency)	Where? (place)	How much? (quantity)
angrily	merrily	afterwards	always	above	almost
anxiously	nervously	again	annually	around	completely
cautiously	quickly	before	constantly	away	entirely
cheerfully	sadly	beforehand	daily	below	little
courageously	safely	early	hourly	down	much
crossly	shyly	lately	monthly	downstairs	rather
cruelly	solemnly	never	never	everywhere	totally
defiantly	weakly	now	occasionally	here	very
doubtfully	well	often	often	inside	
elegantly	wildly	punctually	once	outside	
enthusiastically		recently	regularly	there	
foolishly		soon	repeatedly	up	
frantically		then	sometimes	upstairs	
gently		today	usually	wherever	
gladly		tomorrow	yearly		
gracefully		yesterday			
happily					
hungrily					
inquisitively					
irritably					
joyously					
loudly					
madly					

More useful adverbs...

additionally	appropriately	consequently
fittingly	hence	however
insufficiently	suitably	therefore

Verbs

Movement		Voice	Objects	Emotion	Senses	Thought
bounce	stroll	giggle	bend	admire	caress	comprehend
carry	stumble	hum	break	bawl	eat	conceive
collapse	tap	laugh	burn	blubber	feel	contemplate
crawl	throw	rap	control	cry	hear	daydream
dance	trudge	scream	fold	despair	lick	dream
dash	turn	shout	melt	frown	listen	evaluate
drive	walk	sigh	mend	grin	observe	lament
hit	wander	sing	mould	laugh	smell	meditate
hop	wave	sob	open	love	sniff	ponder
hurry	wind	talk	repair	sigh	taste	reflect
jump	zoom	whisper	smash	smile	touch	speculate
leap		yawn	snap	smirk		think
live			stretch	tremble		visualise
pull			throw	weep		wonder
push			twist	wince		
roll				worry		
rotate						
run						
shake						
skip						
sneak						
spin						
split						

More useful verbs...

change	collect	design	focus	find
identify	locate	plan	prevent	report
suggest	search	select	terminate	visit

My Word Mat

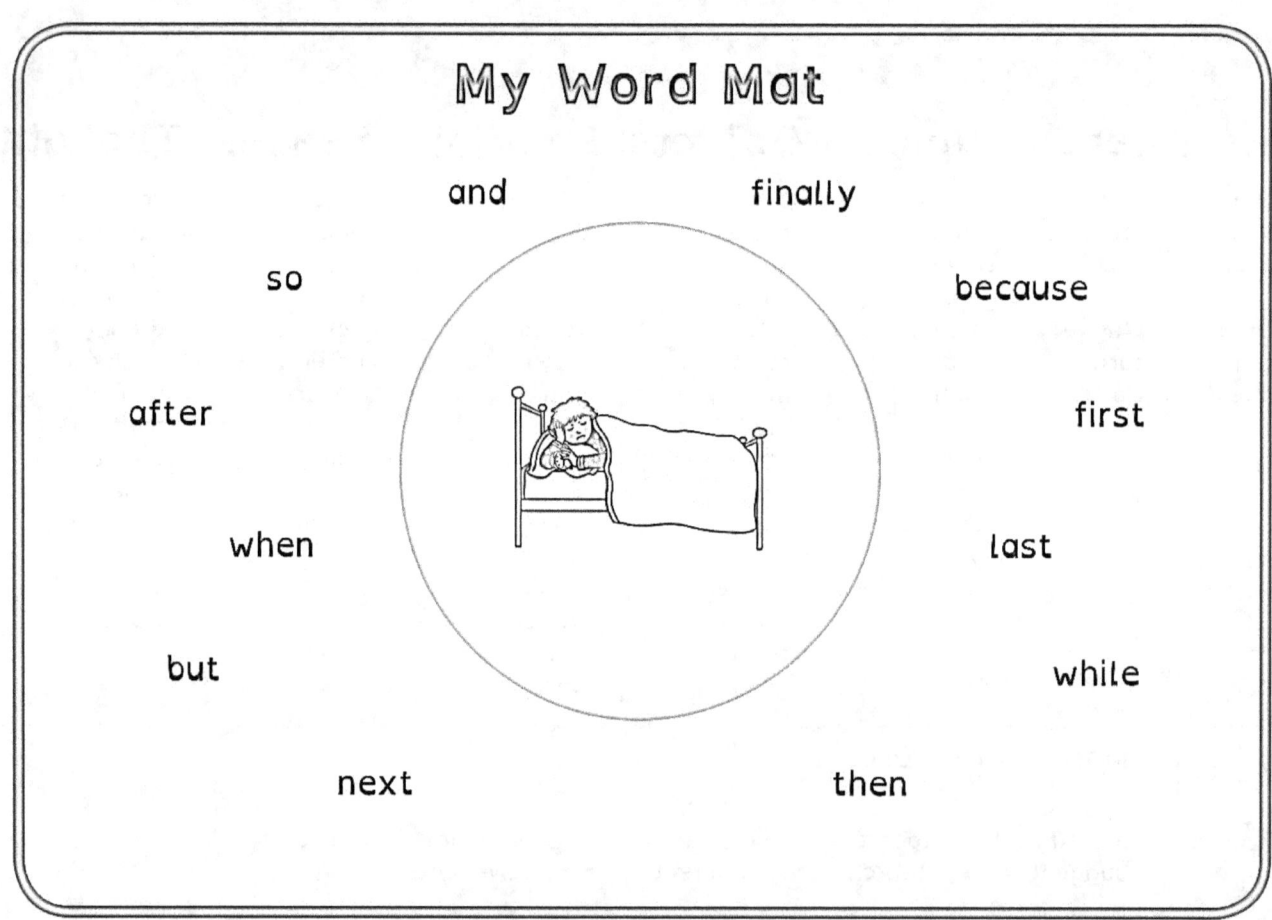

and finally

so because

after first

when last

but while

next then

My Word Mat

and   finally

so   because

after   first

when   last

but   while

next   then

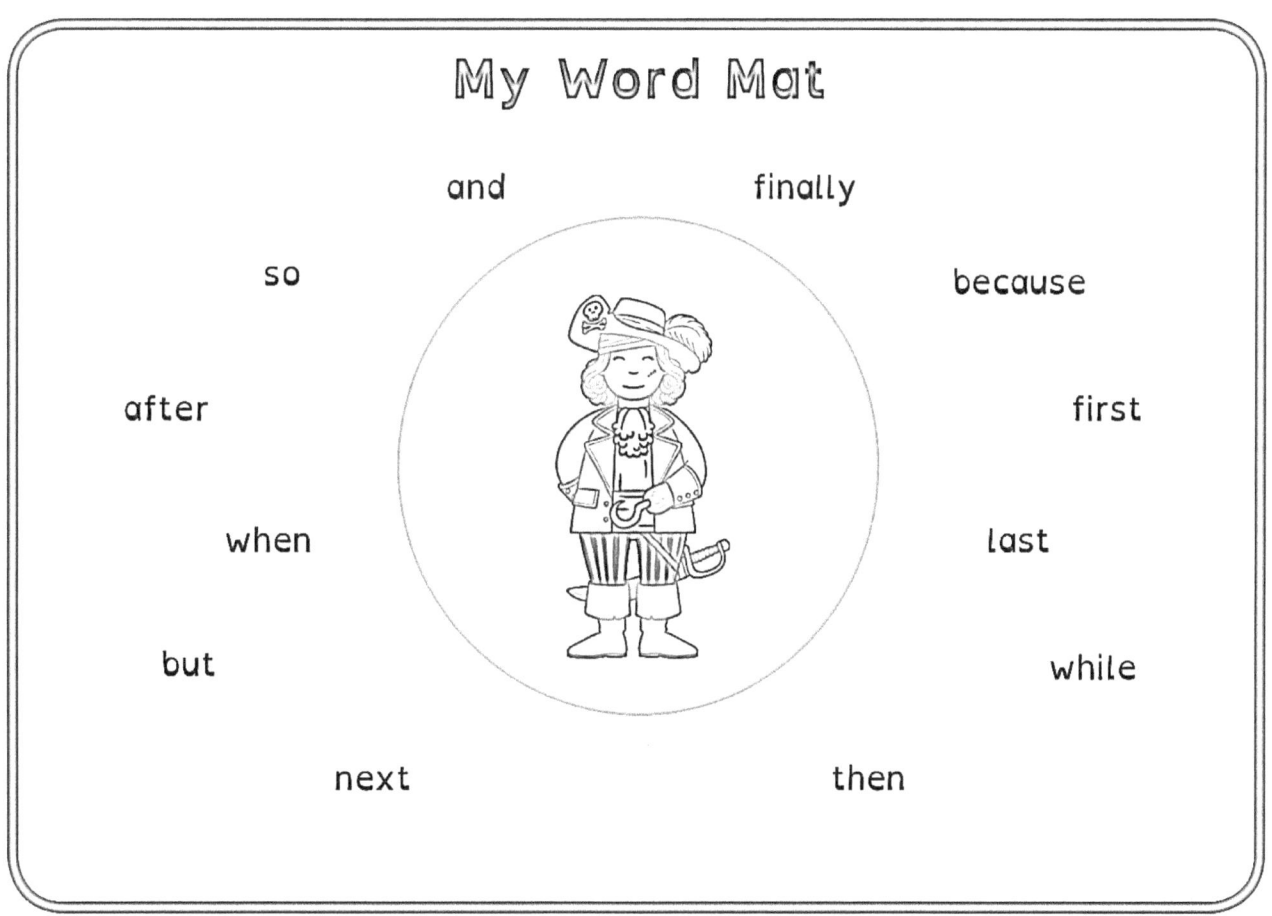

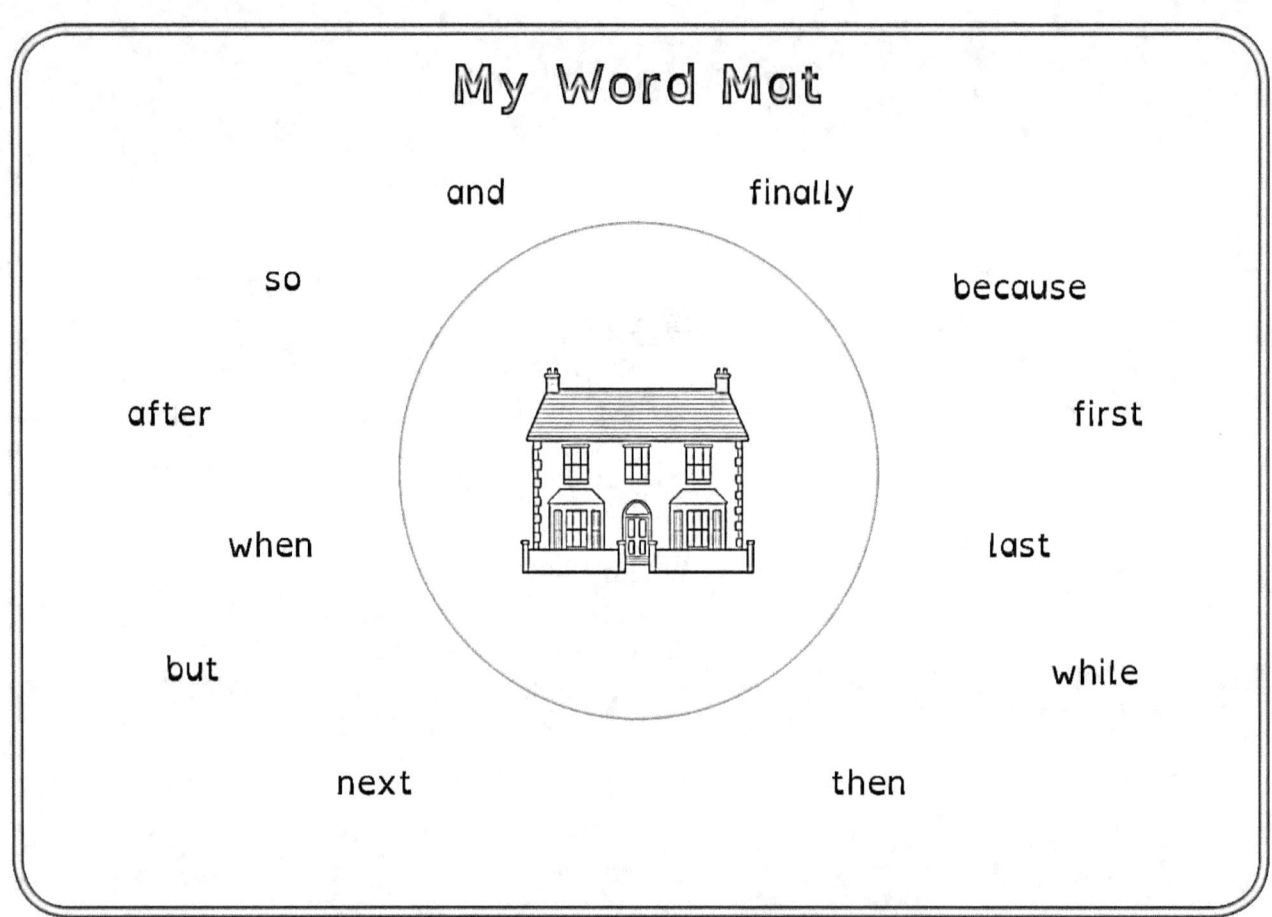

My Word Mat

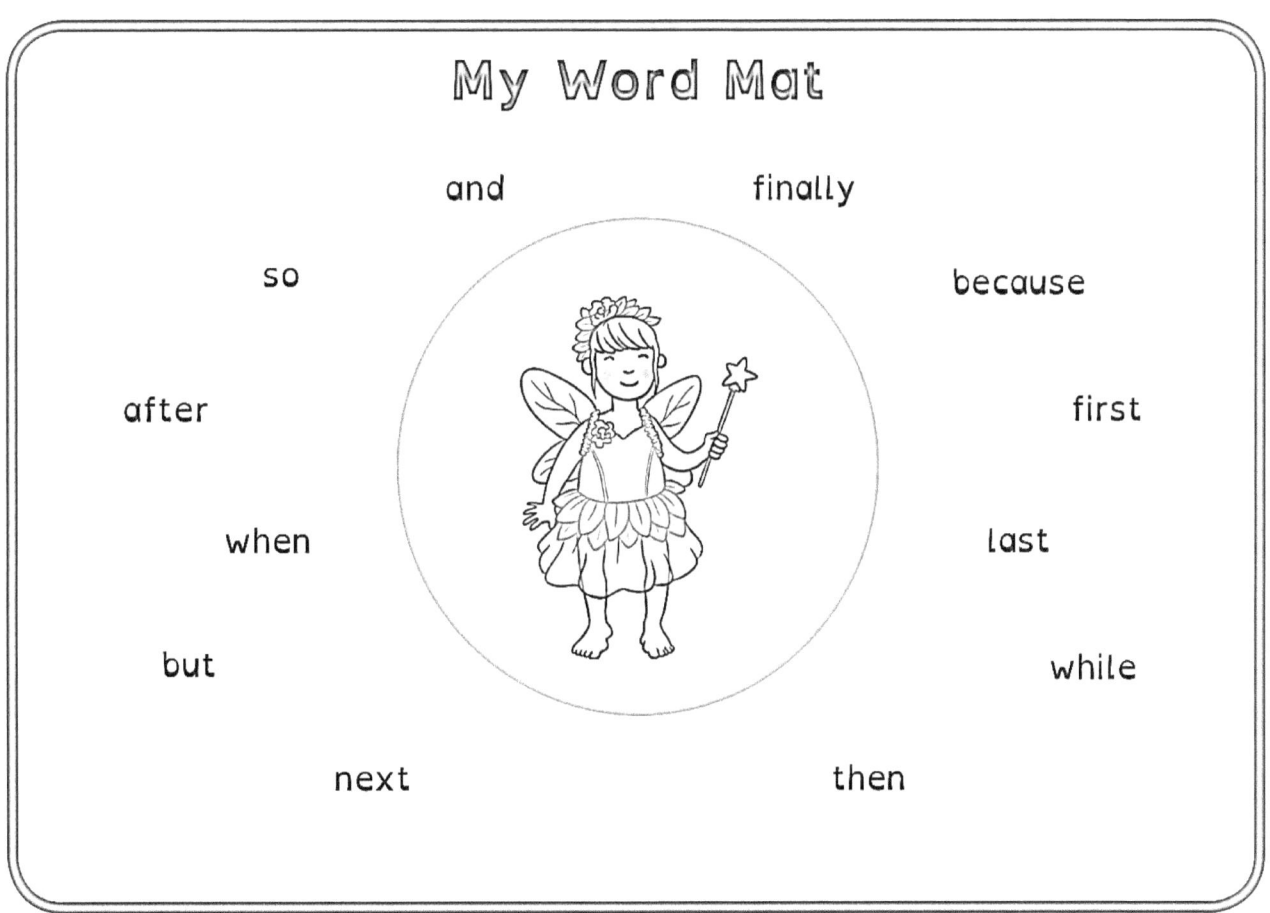

and finally

so because

after first

when last

but while

next then

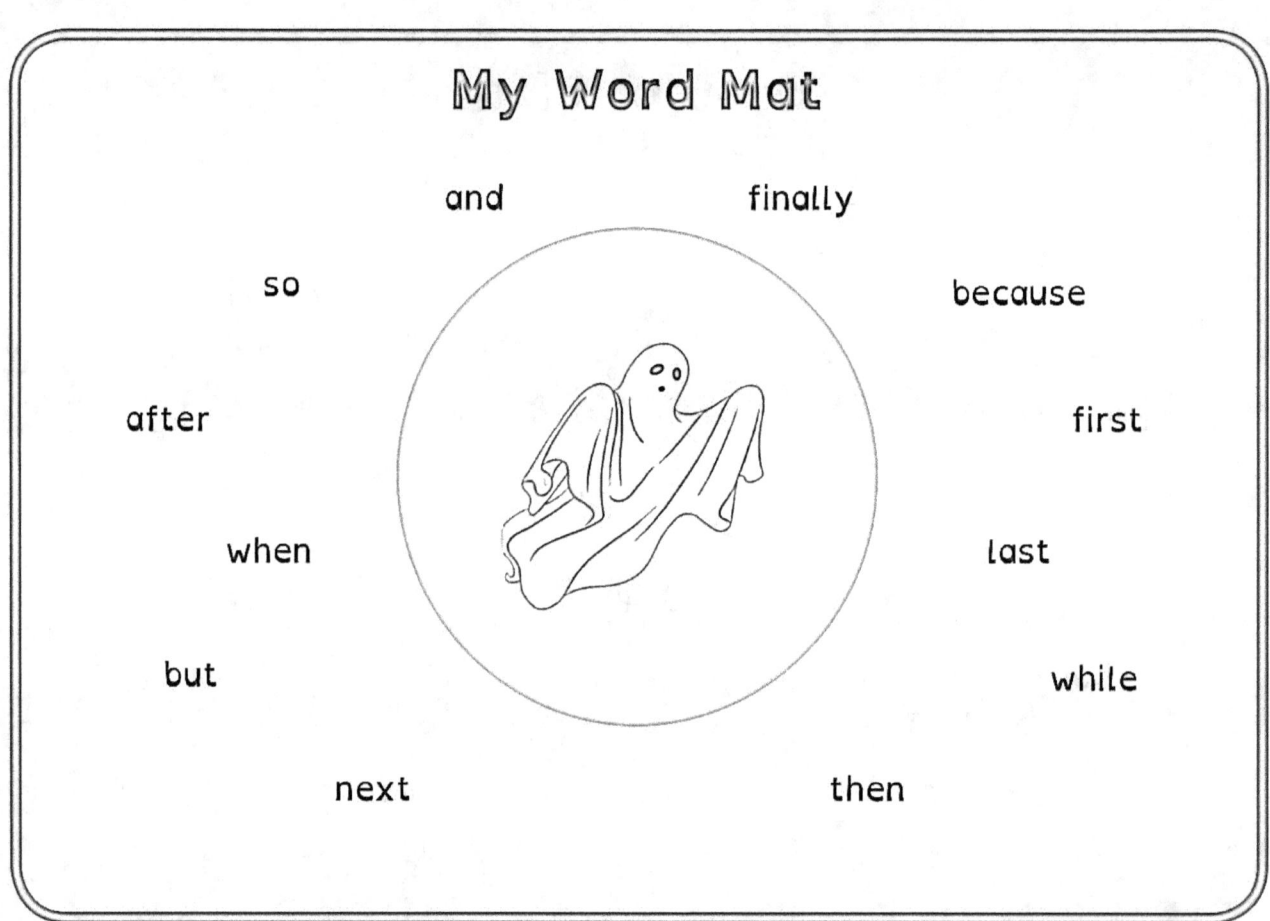

My Word Mat

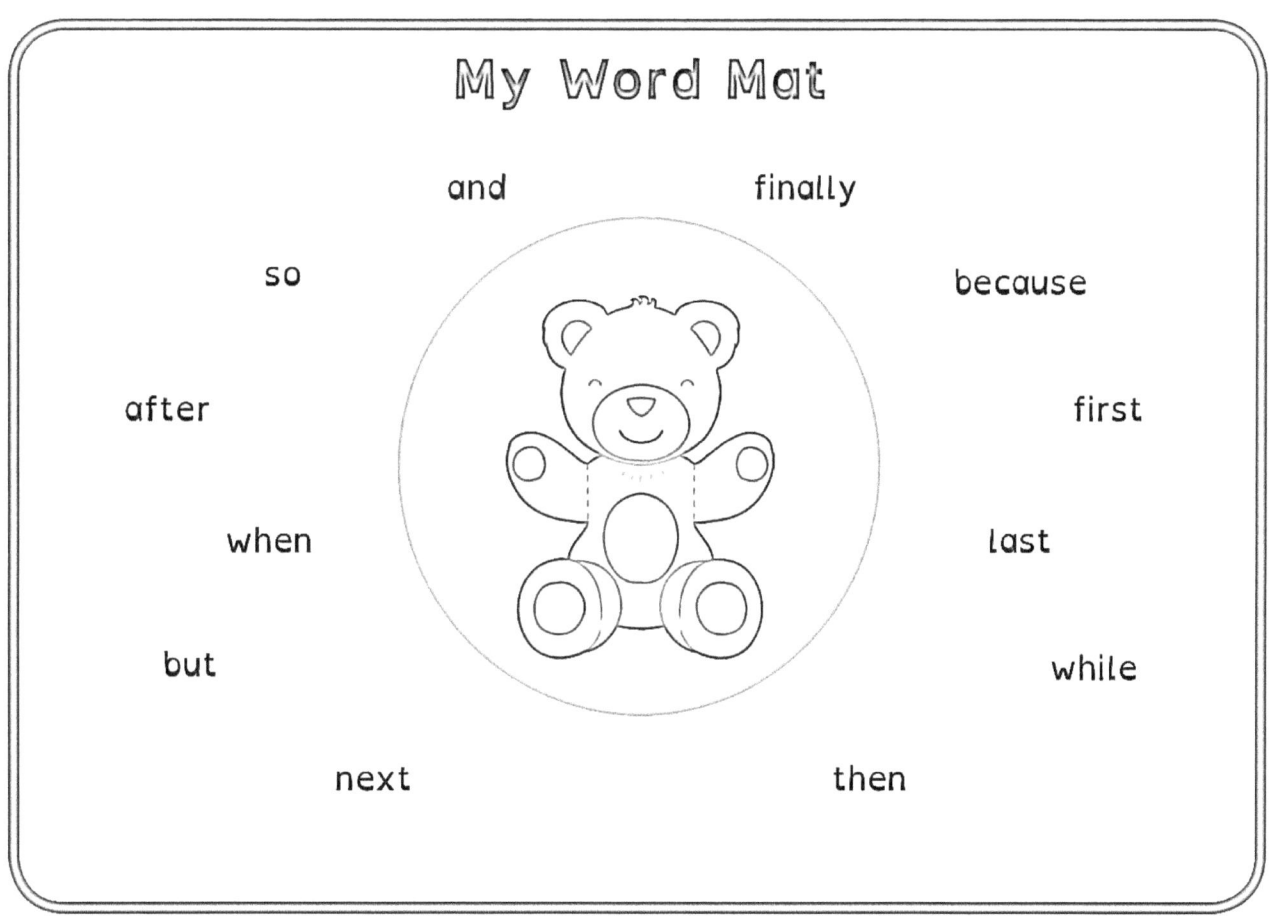

and finally

so because

after first

when last

but while

next then

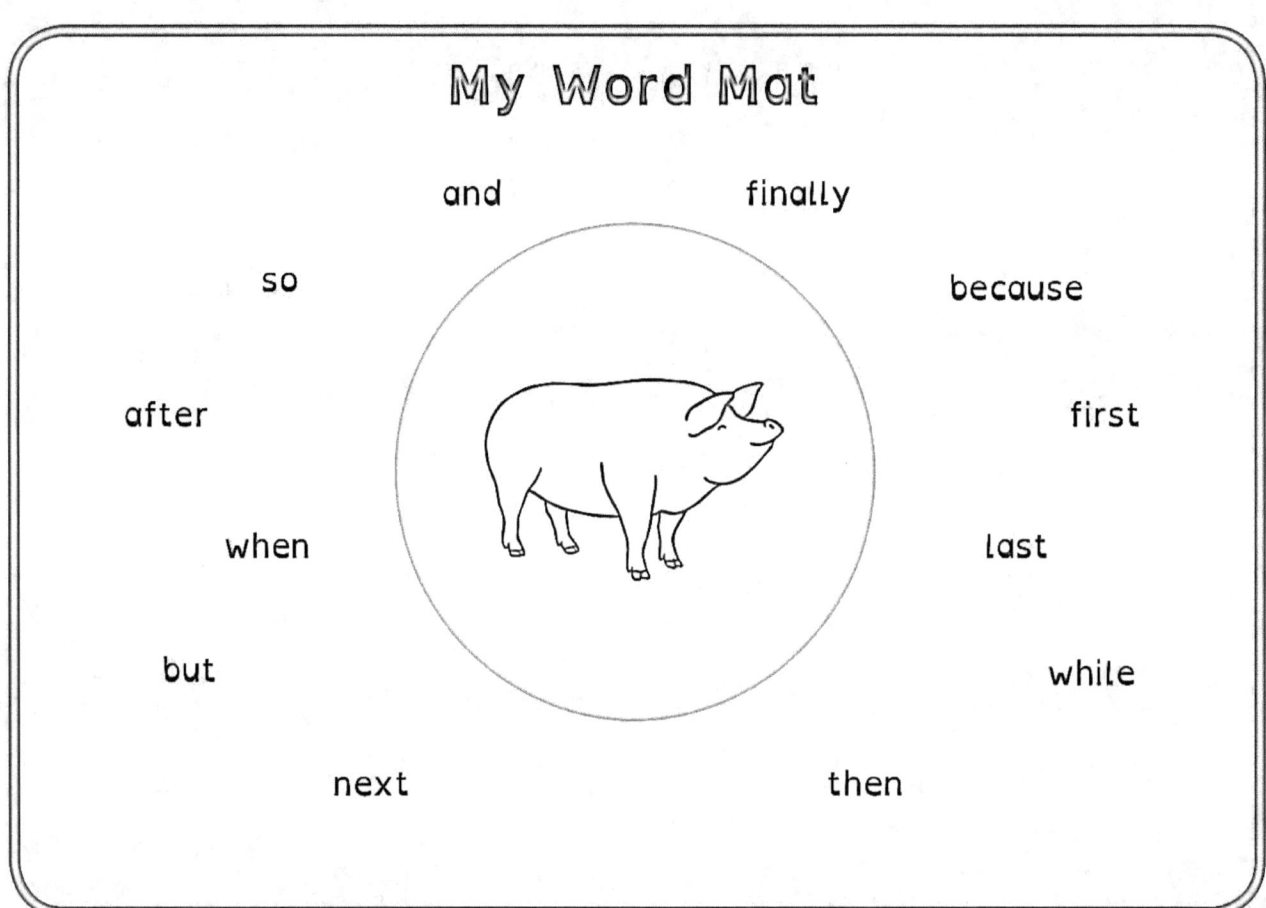

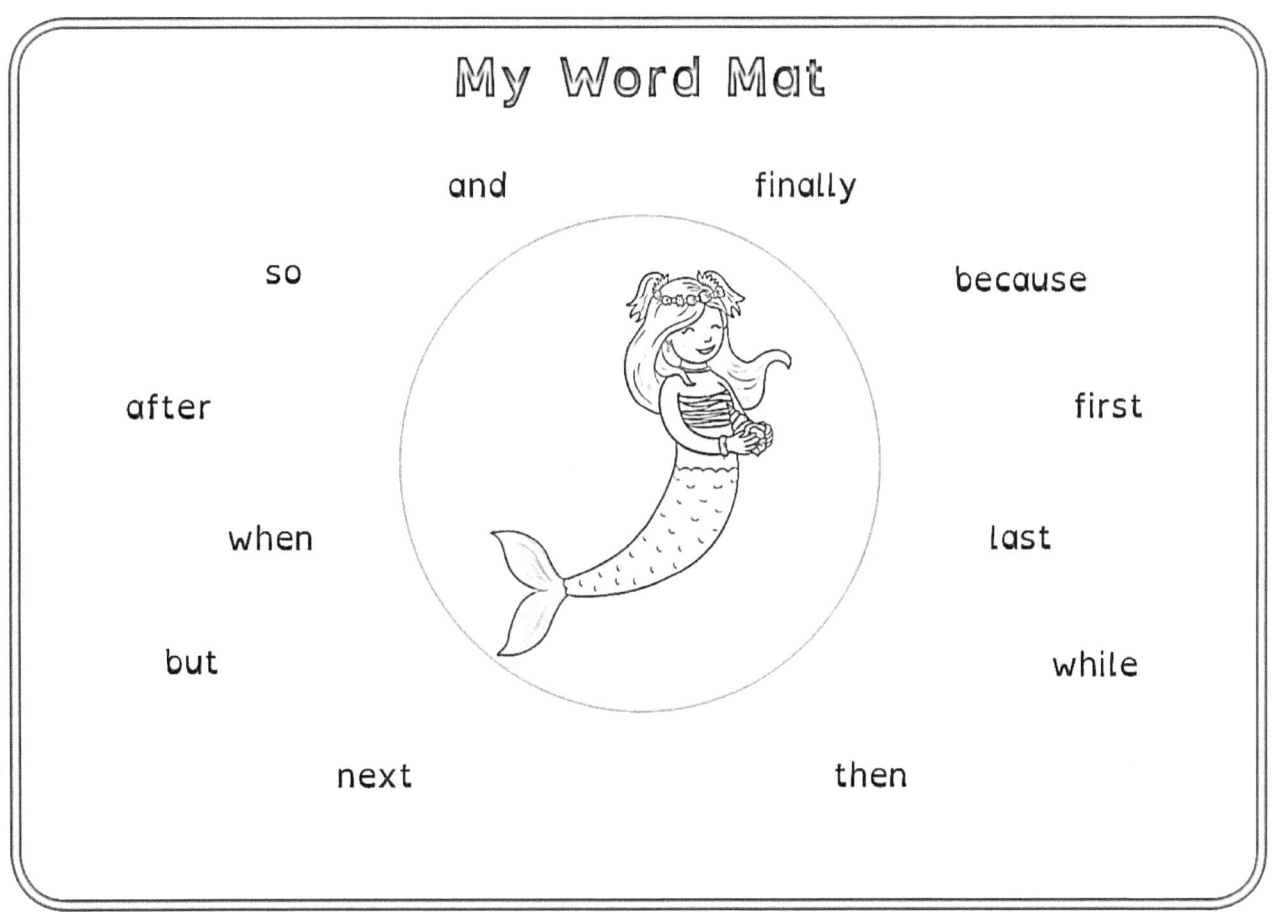

My Word Mat

about	by	good	jump	may	once	so	two
after	call	got	just	more	one	some	us
again	called	had	last	much	or	take	very
an	came	half	laugh	must	our	than	want
another	can't	has	little	name	out	that	water
as	could	have	live	new	over	their	way
back	did	help			people	them	were
ball	do	her			push	then	what
be	don't	here			pull	there	when
because	dig	him	lived	next	put	these	where
bed	door	his	love	night	saw	three	who
been	down	home	made	not	school	time	will
boy	first	house	make	now	seen	too	with
brother	from	how	man	off	should	took	would
but	girl	if	many	old	sister	tree	your

My Word Mat

about	by	good	jump	may	once	so	two
after	call	got	just	more	one	some	us
again	called	had	last	much	or	take	very
an	came	half	laugh	must	our	than	want
another	can't	has	little	name	out	that	water
as	could	have	live	new	over	their	way
back	did	help			people	them	were
ball	do	her			push	then	what
be	don't	here			pull	there	when
because	dig	him	lived	next	put	these	where
bed	door	his	love	night	saw	three	who
been	down	home	made	not	school	time	will
boy	first	house	make	now	seen	too	with
brother	from	how	man	off	should	took	would
but	girl	if	many	old	sister	tree	your

My Word Mat

about	by	good	jump	may	once	so	two
after	call	got	just	more	one	some	us
again	called	had	last	much	or	take	very
an	came	half	laugh	must	our	than	want
another	can't	has	little	name	out	that	water
as	could	have	live	new	over	their	way
back	did	help			people	them	were
ball	do	her			push	then	what
be	don't	here			pull	there	when
because	dig	him	lived	next	put	these	where
bed	door	his	love	night	saw	three	who
been	down	home	made	not	school	time	will
boy	first	house	make	now	seen	too	with
brother	from	how	man	off	should	took	would
but	girl	if	many	old	sister	tree	your

My Word Mat

about	by	good	jump	may	once	so	two
after	call	got	just	more	one	some	us
again	called	had	last	much	or	take	very
an	came	half	laugh	must	our	than	want
another	can't	has	little	name	out	that	water
as	could	have	live	new	over	their	way
back	did	help			people	them	were
ball	do	her			push	then	what
be	don't	here			pull	there	when
because	dig	him	lived	next	put	these	where
bed	door	his	love	night	saw	three	who
been	down	home	made	not	school	time	will
boy	first	house	make	now	seen	too	with
brother	from	how	man	off	should	took	would
but	girl	if	many	old	sister	tree	your

My Word Mat

about	by	good	jump	may	once	so	two
after	call	got	just	more	one	some	us
again	called	had	last	much	or	take	very
an	came	half	laugh	must	our	than	want
another	can't	has	little	name	out	that	water
as	could	have	live	new	over	their	way
back	did	help			people	them	were
ball	do	her			push	then	what
be	don't	here			pull	there	when
because	dig	him	lived	next	put	these	where
bed	door	his	love	night	saw	three	who
been	down	home	made	not	school	time	will
boy	first	house	make	now	seen	too	with
brother	from	how	man	off	should	took	would
but	girl	if	many	old	sister	tree	your

My Word Mat

about	by	good	jump	may	once	so	two
after	call	got	just	more	one	some	us
again	called	had	last	much	or	take	very
an	came	half	laugh	must	our	than	want
another	can't	has	little	name	out	that	water
as	could	have	live	new	over	their	way
back	did	help			people	them	were
ball	do	her			push	then	what
be	don't	here			pull	there	when
because	dig	him	lived	next	put	these	where
bed	door	his	love	night	saw	three	who
been	down	home	made	not	school	time	will
boy	first	house	make	now	seen	too	with
brother	from	how	man	off	should	took	would
but	girl	if	many	old	sister	tree	your

My Word Mat

about	by	good	jump	may	once	so	two
after	call	got	just	more	one	some	us
again	called	had	last	much	or	take	very
an	came	half	laugh	must	our	than	want
another	can't	has	little	name	out	that	water
as	could	have	live	new	over	their	way
back	did	help			people	them	were
ball	do	her			push	then	what
be	don't	here			pull	there	when
because	dig	him	lived	next	put	these	where
bed	door	his	love	night	saw	three	who
been	down	home	made	not	school	time	will
boy	first	house	make	now	seen	too	with
brother	from	how	man	off	should	took	would
but	girl	if	many	old	sister	tree	your

My Word Mat

about	by	good	jump	may	once	so	two
after	call	got	just	more	one	some	us
again	called	had	last	much	or	take	very
an	came	half	laugh	must	our	than	want
another	can't	has	little	name	out	that	water
as	could	have	live	new	over	their	way
back	did	help			people	them	were
ball	do	her			push	then	what
be	don't	here			pull	there	when
because	dig	him	lived	next	put	these	where
bed	door	his	love	night	saw	three	who
been	down	home	made	not	school	time	will
boy	first	house	make	now	seen	too	with
brother	from	how	man	off	should	took	would
but	girl	if	many	old	sister	tree	your

My Word Mat

about	by	good	jump	may	once	so	two
after	call	got	just	more	one	some	us
again	called	had	last	much	or	take	very
an	came	half	laugh	must	our	than	want
another	can't	has	little	name	out	that	water
as	could	have	live	new	over	their	way
back	did	help			people	them	were
ball	do	her			push	then	what
be	don't	here		next	pull	there	when
because	dig	him	lived	night	put	these	where
bed	door	his	love	not	saw	three	who
been	down	home	made	now	school	time	will
boy	first	house	make	off	seen	too	with
brother	from	how	man	old	should	took	would
but	girl	if	many		sister	tree	your

My Word Mat

about	by	good	jump	may	once	so	two
after	call	got	just	more	one	some	us
again	called	had	last	much	or	take	very
an	came	half	laugh	must	our	than	want
another	can't	has	little	name	out	that	water
as	could	have	live	new	over	their	way
back	did	help			people	them	were
ball	do	her			push	then	what
be	don't	here			pull	there	when
because	dig	him	lived	next	put	these	where
bed	door	his	love	night	saw	three	who
been	down	home	made	not	school	time	will
boy	first	house	make	now	seen	too	with
brother	from	how	man	off	should	took	would
but	girl	if	many	old	sister	tree	your

My Word Mat

about	by	good	jump	may	once	so	two
after	call	got	just	more	one	some	us
again	called	had	last	much	or	take	very
an	came	half	laugh	must	our	than	want
another	can't	has	little	name	out	that	water
as	could	have	live	new	over	their	way
back	did	help			people	them	were
ball	do	her			push	then	what
be	don't	here			pull	there	when
because	dig	him	lived	next	put	these	where
bed	door	his	love	night	saw	three	who
been	down	home	made	not	school	time	will
boy	first	house	make	now	seen	too	with
brother	from	how	man	off	should	took	would
but	girl	if	many	old	sister	tree	your

My Word Mat

about	by	good	jump	may	once	so	two
after	call	got	just	more	one	some	us
again	called	had	last	much	or	take	very
an	came	half	laugh	must	our	than	want
another	can't	has	little	name	out	that	water
as	could	have	live	new	over	their	way
back	did	help			people	them	were
ball	do	her			push	then	what
be	don't	here			pull	there	when
because	dig	him	lived	next	put	these	where
bed	door	his	love	night	saw	three	who
been	down	home	made	not	school	time	will
boy	first	house	make	now	seen	too	with
brother	from	how	man	off	should	took	would
but	girl	if	many	old	sister	tree	your

My Tricky Letters and Sounds Word Mat

Aa all are asked any	Bb be because	Cc come called could	Dd do different	Ee eyes	Ff for friends	Gg go	Hh he her have	Ii I into
Ll like little looked laughed	Mm me my Mr Mrs many mouse	Nn no	Oo one out oh once	Pp people please	Ss she said so some	Tt the to they their thought through	Ww we was were when what water where who work	Yy you

ar	oi	ch	qu	ure	cc	ai	oa
or	ear	sh	er	ow	ff	ee	zz
ur	air	th	ng	oo	ll	igh	

Aa Bb Cc Dd Ee Ff Gg Hh Ii Jj Kk Ll Mm Nn Oo Pp Qq Rr Ss Tt Uu Vv Ww Xx Yy Zz

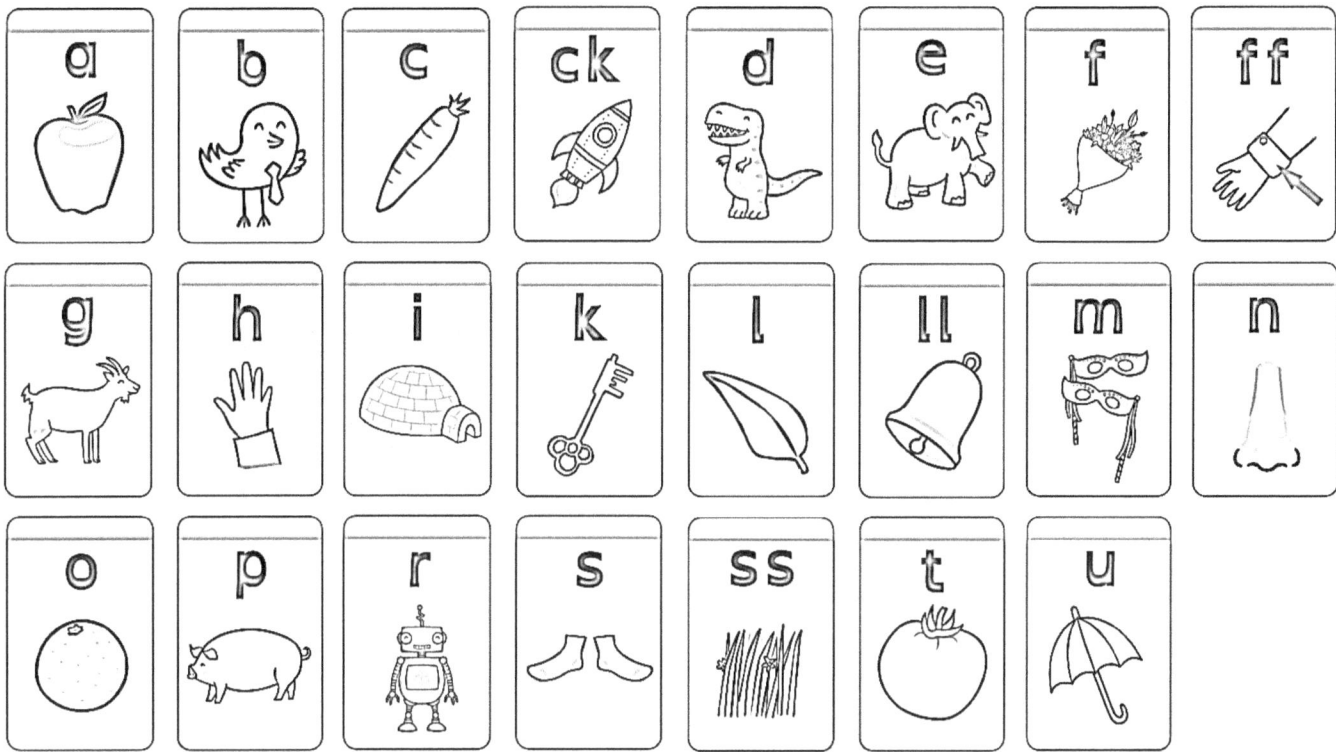
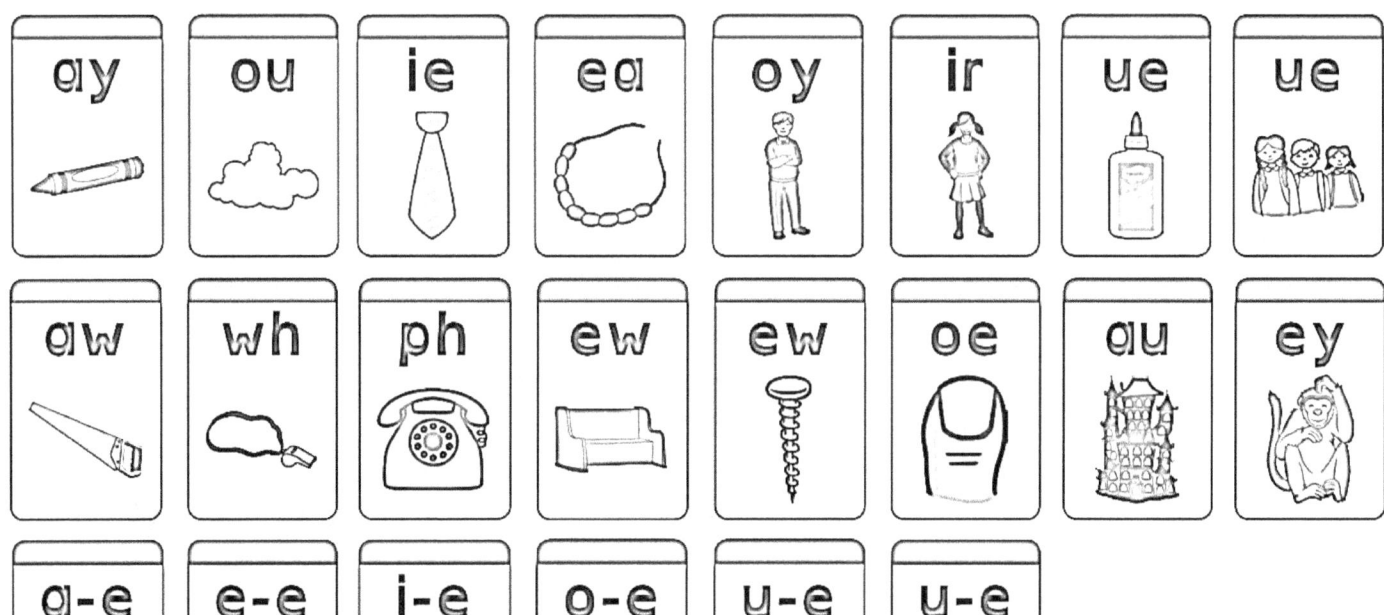

Thank you!
Please leave a review.

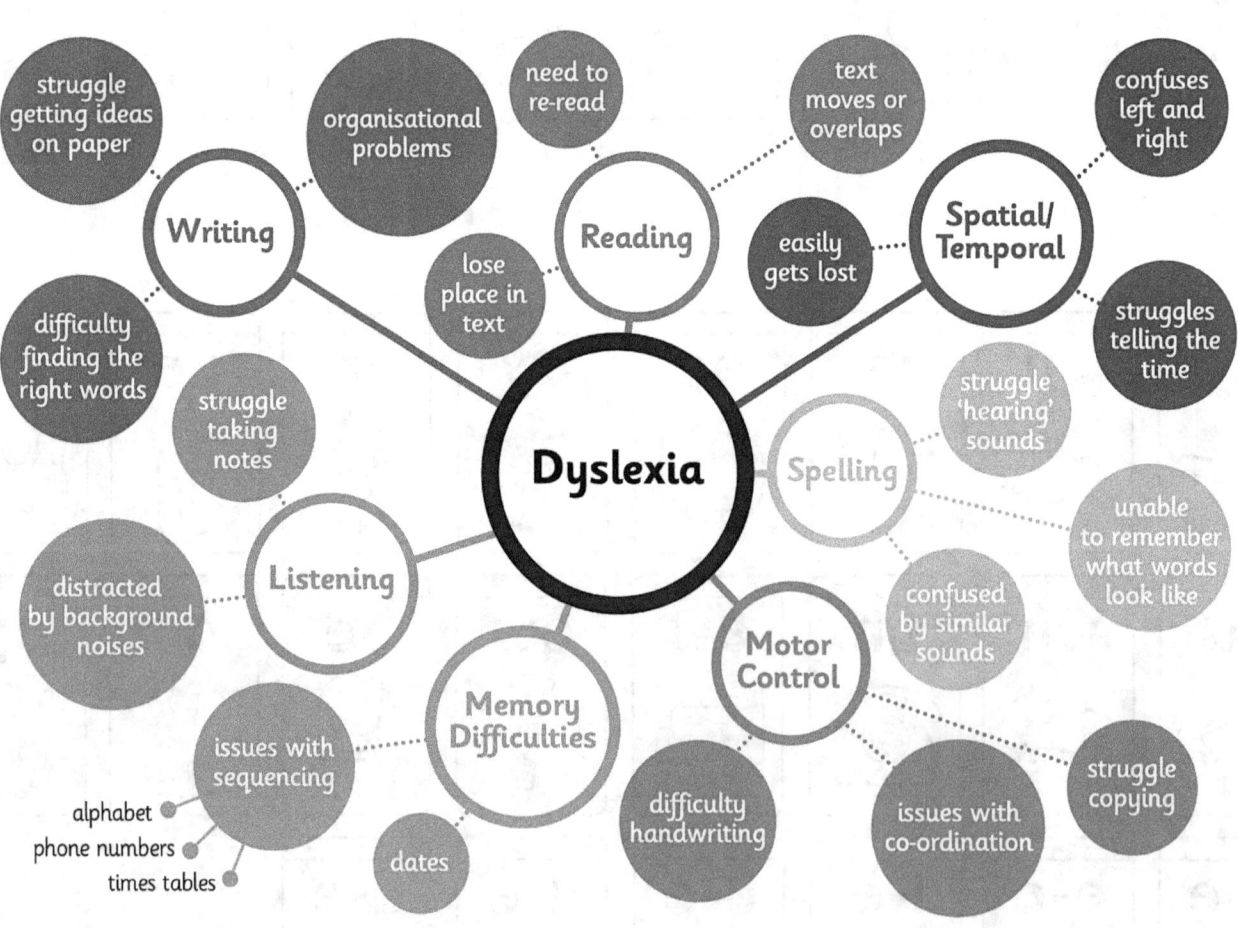